exhume

B. Medina

To my brother, Joshie.

contents

(pre)

I

(inter)

II

(post)

(pre)

Rhythm's been damned

let us swim into the daze days

when we retire ire
to Nether isles
for idle thinkings;

mint thoughts
into beveled coins
for restless hands
to possess metal immobile lands
with solitary fights,
mights
too godly for innocuous Earth.

I

Dearest Drones,

bend a dream, Drone.
you can't.

strike a sky, Drone,
to the black.
blue and sand towns – way past.

abandon queenly abodes, Drone.
col lapse
hex a gonal domes – pull back.

bend a dream, Drone.
you can't
transfuse blood to your electric sleep.

volantes

like fierce volantes_we ride
pot hole as phalt skies.

violent with class less freedom_we a wake
when brightest Sol aligns our glaring ways.

amid arid time dips_we drop and drop and drop into thigh flesh sting
car seat pops.

Wheat Land Pill Grims

to the West there is More Land
for ill pill grim wanderers.

hill lands of wheat
reserved for the high Hampton markets
roll along chalk muraled banks
of waterway streets.

gold plated led platforms
with crates of opera glasses
free for the 2-minute using
rise and fall and drift in slights.

corpus trains float on.
they breathe – they do not live.
they move rolling eyes – they do not blink.
they stretch i.v.y pricked hands and arms to – they never reach –
a bastard sky with no king.

corpus trains float on
in candy damned caskets
of minced cottonwood branches,
bits caramelized into five face coffins.

corpus trains float on
in the padding of dotted garment gowns
for the unaccompanied incontinent.

Corpus
in the crystalline slop
of the (auto)biographical Before
preceding in sped brief
the deep black After.

Painting Knives

on the lake bridge with the toll,

Desert Sky hitches rides on trunks of hatchbacks
in the primed patches of our metal hoods.

back to Lunatic East, we,
in our three piece suits,
smuggle pieces of our savage mistress.

The Saints of Garden Parties

manzanas rotas levántenos

descansando en la tierra,
después de la junta en el jardín,
bocas vino infectaron a manzanas ya rotas.

manzanas rotas levántenos

hangover hobbyists
planted by butlers and maids
took root in the backyard chalk fields.

manzanas rotas levántenos

by morning breaks,
it was sad to see,
veritas cotton bits hematomized
in the walls of defunct wine mouths.

and all went as well as planned.

misplaced beds

bound to reclining chairs

we'll meet the cut sun

to lay down our ashen likenesses
in attic lune coffins.

infancies

infancies.
to tattoo lined paper with
pencil pricks gliding on
eraser filaments.

infancies.
a kin to
a rising rubble
and fast falls of
our clear sky skins.

no. infancies.
to dismember that wire of the ether
from we growing caged cable peoples.

(inter)

asphalt, live.

- nomadic unknown flash motion.
- need roots for nausea.
- one label to fill solid chameleonic tendencies.

II

arch

we're at home
in laundromats and arcades.

adults, children, machines.
quarters and tokens.
washing and competing.
drying and screaming.

let's fold time and switch.
i'll be the quarter.
you'll be the token.

alva stains

she had on that makemeblush
lipstick and kissed me once.

kerosene rosetree taste
waxes slick
my oncecelibate lips;

helps me whistle myself higher to
the plains of blues so
I may climb and
hop clouds

all the way down the southern valley to overlook the motherland that
bleeds for ends to
greed and addictions.

sleep

No dreams tonight;
only black sleep

and a full moon that will not
light up the telephone pole's embers
with the orange glow
of beaten molten iron;

nor fumigate the roads of masses
with their whittled chalk piece
of yellow sulfur.

She will keep my sleeping embers tonight. Sleeping splinters will not spark,
nor light the street blocks of
telephone poles
tattooed behind my eyelids.

No speaking tonight
with the one I love
across wires.

No burning into
colliding smiles
in those Technicolor/neuronfires.

I may only sink
into blackest sleep.

short film

I see you
standing in film strip blue rooms.

As naked as negative space you move.
An 8mm glow displacing blue.

I see you
advancing in film strip blue rooms.

Like candy shell gloss coats
you exhale sugar fumes.
White figure space in motion.
Your speeding frames
bring me closer to you.

I see you
over exposing in film strip blue rooms.

Hot Envy Lens dish
steals and subsumes you
as a live piece incubating
in its rust specimen collection.

refuge

me at my observation post
treading sleep in these mountains.
my bowing lashes
like a centipede among lush blue
weighing down my eyelids.

we on this freight train
wading through neutral night.
our boxcar bodies
like a centipede among lush blue
weighing down eyes of ordered post men.

trees

A lonely pair of bark lungs breathed in
the invisible o's floating everywhere.

With each inhalation,
the wire from the fence
stretched and pricked them;

it fell and curled,
rounding up and to the left,
like a ribbon
after the two-armed blade
slides along it.

And the metal filaments filtered through and gripped them and held
them still until they couldn't sigh or grasp on.

But they left
in the clear space
between all the houses and cats and dogs and furniture and people,

compound gases that gripped us tight,
so our chests did not rise and fall;
so that we did not stain
pocket-sized mirrors with hot vapor;

so that we stood still and fell straight down when we were hacked
away by bearded monsters laughing and yelling timber.

elective

we were confused

when our humanitarian studies professor put away her chalk piece
and turned out the lights.

two images appeared
on the white walls
damaged by our campus's frequent rains.

to our right –
"black branded duck
deflocked to
salty wave ponds."

to our left –
"coyote's pup
abandoned in
turquoise desert night."

The paint curdled
and peeled
and fell off the wall
in scraps,

leaving
the coyote and the duck
and fifty students
wondering why this class
is listed as a blow off elective.

Yellow's Between Red and Green

ready?

notice this.
the family who lives in the yellow house,
they faked their own death.

the six hundred square feet's amber,
it breathes in constant
along the kitchen window
above the sink
and behind that fruitless pecan tree
that's high enough
so their shadows won't be seen.

everyone there now
didn't know each other then, in life.

the dead find themselves
in the yellow house

floating and consuming each other
's talks and
not so commendable past walks and
cutis sheddings and filth stalks they
grew as extra limbs when they
lived as unreachable fixtures

in other
houses, commuter trains, and offices, and in
needleambrosiademmyvikyflame boxes
like looters with nearby residences desecrating minds
and killing claims to life.

Strange Relative

Tengo una cosa.
Tengo esta cosa.
Me gusta, no,
tengo que,
a veces solo puedo,

escribir en una ventana peculiar
encima de un escritor metal o
descansando en un par de piernas
carnosas – las mías coloradas o
las prietas arrugadas de mi muchacho abuela.

Una ventana siempre blanca,
haciéndose viuda cada otro segundo, cuando la línea difunto
parpadea
como el metrónomo irregular de mi
religión displacida.

Con demasiado marcador alrededor
y en mis ojos,
pasare por siempre mis días
coleccionando flores y tejando manteles.

Esperare esa conversación que tendríamos en la madrugada
cuando, por fin, te podría ver
sentada y parada y paseando,
filtrando la vida
por su propia ventana.

(post)

men of moths

of all the moths and men and mothers
who will care to be there

to dispose of all the clothes in piles darkness left
by crepuscular disappearances

disappeared mourning mothers moth flock moth mothers gnaw at
bulbous altars fluorescing searchingsearchingsearching through hemp
denimflannelsilknylon fabric

hole ingestions just won't do

some day we disappeared will reappear
in the veins hide water marks
in the moth wings manmen abandoned

mothers we used to know wait for morning to finally sleep in hallway
coat closets

ABOUT THE AUTHOR

B. Medina was born and raised in Dallas, TX. She currently resides in the North Texas area and is completing her undergraduate work in English and Mexican-American Studies. *exhume* is her second self-published small volume of poetry. Her first book, *The Talking Room: A Collection of Poems*, was published in 2013. She can be reached at **montemedina.stellarprints@gmail.com**.

www.ingramcontent.com/pod-product-compliance
Lightning Source LLC
Chambersburg PA
CBHW020447030426

42337CB00014B/1435